To: Payton
Happy reading!
Love,
Rylan, Reyna, Royden
Uncle Bruce &
Aunty Iris
10/31/2006

ALOHA!
'RUMBLE RUMBLE'
—GAVIN

There's a Monster in My 'Ōpū

Written by
Karyn Hopper

Illustrated by
Gavin Kobayashi

BESS
PRESS

3565 Harding Avenue • Honolulu, Hawaii 96816
Toll Free: (800) 910-2377 • Phone: (808) 734-7159 • Fax: (808) 732-3627
Email: info@besspress.com
www.besspress.com

Library of Congress Cataloging-in-Publication Data

Hopper, Karyn.
 There's a monster in my opu /
Karyn Hopper ; illustrated by
Gavin Kobayashi.
        p. cm.
 Includes illustrations.
 ISBN 1-57306-244-8
1. Ice cream, ices, etc. – Juvenile
fiction. 2. North Shore Region (Oahu,
Hawaii) – Juvenile fiction. 3. Hawaii –
Juvenile fiction. I. Kobayashi, Gavin.
II. Title.
PZ7.H67 2006   [E]-dc21

Copyright 2006 by Bess Press, Inc.

10 09 08 07 06   5 4 3 2 1

Printed in Korea

There's a Monster in My 'Ōpū

For Billy,
who taught me
the meaning
of aloha

- Karyn

And for
Melanie,
Hunter-Logan
and
Hudson-Clark

- Gavin

There's a monster in my 'ōpū.
He's impossible to see.
I heard him there this morning
When he growled a "Growl" at me.

Rumble Gurgle
Rumble Growl
Rumble Burble-dee!

Cloudless skies and Saturday,
A perfect time for sun.
My daddy packed me on his bike.
My monster joined the fun.

We biked through Haleʻiwa,
Where the tourists come to play.
We pedaled ʻcross the Rainbow Bridge
And smelled the ocean spray.

Rumble
Gurgle

Rumble
Growl

Rumble
Burble-dee!

We spent the sunny morning
Surfing on the sea,
Chasing sand crabs to their holes
And catching two or three.

My shorts dripped salty water
As I climbed a sandy mound.
I spun a cartwheel to the shore
And laughed as I rolled down.

Blub. Blub. Glub. Glub.
My monster roared at me.
We rested in the shade
Of a giant North Shore tree.

Rumble
Gurgle

Rumble
Growl

Rumble
Burble-dee!

I dreamed of crabs and surfboards.
(Was my monster sleeping now?)
He rumbled and he grumbled
'Til I knew my nap was pau.

Rumble Gurgle

Rumble Growl

Rumble Burble-dee!

We stopped to say "Aloha!"
To my auntie by the sea.
She put away her haku lei
And blew a kiss to me.

She looked down at my ʻōpū
And chuckled at the noise.
She tucked some money in my hand,
"For Matsumoto's, boys."

Rumble
Gurgle

Rumble
Growl

Rumble
Burble-dee!

My monster sped us back to town.
We saw a welcome sign.
We rushed into the little shop
And shuffled through the line.

"Lychee, mango, coconut.
Make it large today!"
I slurped the shave ice to the cone . . .